KU-428-645

Stories from Faiths

ISLAM

Rohail Aslam

Schools Library and Information Services

S00000722582

www.heinemannlibrary.co.uk
Visit our website to find out more information about Heinemann Library books.

To order:
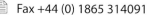
☎ Phone +44 (0) 1865 888066
🖹 Fax +44 (0) 1865 314091
🖵 Visit www.heinemannlibrary.co.uk

Heinemann Library is an imprint of Capstone Global Library Limited, a company incorporated in England and Wales having its registered office at 7 Pilgrim Street, London, EC4V 6LB – Registered company number: 6695582

"Heinemann" is a registered trademark of Pearson Education Limited, under licence to Capstone Global Library Limited

Text © Capstone Global Library Limited 2008
First published in hardback in 2009
Paperback edition first published in 2010

The moral rights of the proprietor have been asserted.

All rights reserved. No part of this publication may be reproduced in any form or by any means (including photocopying or storing it in any medium by electronic means and whether or not transiently or incidentally to some other use of this publication) without the written permission of the copyright owner, except in accordance with the provisions of the Copyright, Designs and Patents Act 1988 or under the terms of a licence issued by the Copyright Licensing Agency, Saffron House, 6–10 Kirby Street, London EC1N 8TS (www.cla.co.uk). Applications for the copyright owner's written permission should be addressed to the publisher.

Designer: Harleen Mehta
Picture Researchers: Dimple Bhorwal, S Kripa
Art Director: Rahul Dhiman
Client Service Manager: Aparna Malhotra
Project Manager: Smita Mehta, Santosh Vasudevan
Lineart: Sibi N Devasia
Colouring Artists: Subhash Vohra, Danish Zaidi, Ashish Tanwa
Originated by Chroma Graphics (Overseas) Pte Ltd
Printed and bound in China by CTPS

ISBN 978-0-431-08223-3 (hardback)
13 12 11 10 09
10 9 8 7 6 5 4 3 2 1

ISBN 978-0-431-08230-1 (paperback)
14 13 12 11 10
10 9 8 7 6 5 4 3 2 1

British Library Cataloguing in Publication Data
Aslam, Rohail
    Islam. – (Stories from faiths)
    297
A full catalogue record for this book is available from the British Library.

Acknowledgements

We would like to thank the following for permission to reproduce photographs (t = top, b = bottom, c = centre, l = left, r = right, m = middle): Salem Alforaih/ Shutterstock: 4b, Ali Mubarak/ Photolibrary: 5b, Anson Hung/ Shutterstock: 7tr, J. Helgason/ Shutterstock: 8tl, Images&Stories/ Alamy: 11tr, Jodi Jacobson/ iStockphoto: 12tl, A.M Faruqui/ The Hindu: 15tr, K Murali Kumar/ The Hindu: 16tl, Helene Rogers/ Alamy: 19tr, Frans Lemmens/ Alamy: 20tl, Hilly Collective/ iStockphoto: 23tr, Salamanderman/ Shutterstock: 24tl, Manojmundapat/ Dreamstime: 27tr, B.K Bangash/ Associated Press: 28tl.

Q2A Media Art Bank: 6–7, 8–9, 10–11, 13, 14–15, 17, 18, 20–21, 22, 24–25, 26–27, 29.

Cover photograph of a Muslim boy praying reproduced with permission of Paul Thuysbaert/ Photolibrary.

We would like to thank Q2AMEDIA for invaluable help in the preparation of this book.

Every effort has been made to contact copyright holders of material reproduced in this book. Any omissions will be rectified in subsequent printings if notice is given to the publishers.

Disclaimer

All the Internet addresses (URLs) given in this book were valid at the time of going to press. However, due to the dynamic nature of the Internet, some addresses may have changed, or sites may have changed or ceased to exist since publication. While the author and publishers regret any inconvenience this may cause readers, no responsibility for any such changes can be accepted by either the author or the publishers.

DUDLEY PUBLIC LIBRARIES
L
722582   &H
        J 297

Contents

NOTE

When Muslims use the name of the Prophet Muhammad, they usually follow it with the blessing 'Peace be upon him'. In this book the blessing appears as an abbreviation (pbuh).

Some words are printed in bold, **like this**. You can find out what they mean in the glossary.

What is Islam?

The word *Islam* means "obedience to God". People who follow the religion of Islam are called Muslims. Muslims believe that there is one God called Allah who created everything – the planets and stars and all living things. The religion of Islam was first spread in a city called **Makkah** in Arabia (now Saudi Arabia) by a man named Muhammad (pbuh), who was chosen by Allah to be His **Prophet**.

Muslims have a holy book called the **Qur'an**, which is a guide that tells Muslims what they should believe and how to live their lives. There are many stories about the prophets in the Qur'an that are also mentioned in the Bible (the holy book of Christians) and the Torah (the holy book of Jews).

This mosque in Makkah is called Masjid Al-Nabawi. It was originally built by Muhammad (pbuh) in the grounds of his house. It is also the site of his grave, which is directly beneath the green dome.

Prophets such as Ibrahim (Abraham), Musa (Moses) and Yusuf (Joseph) are believed in by Islam, Judaism and Christianity. However, the stories of their lives are different in each religion's history.

There are five duties called the **Five Pillars of Islam** that every Muslim must try to fulfil during their life if they can. These are: to believe that there is no God except Allah and that Muhammad (pbuh) is Allah's messenger, to pray five times a day, to help the poor and needy, to **fast** during **Ramadan** and to go on a **pilgrimage** to Makkah at least once.

Islam has now spread to every part of the world and is one of the most popular religions in the world.

In mosques all over the world, Muslims come together not only to pray, but also to sit and read from the Qur'an.

How Allah Created the World

Allah made the great sky, the stars and planets in seven days. On the first and second day, Allah created our planet, Earth. At first, the heavens and the Earth were joined together as one, but Allah separated them and shaped the Earth so that it was round.

The fruit tree in the Garden of Eden was the one plant that Allah forbade Adam and Eve to eat from.

Allah covered the Earth in vast oceans of water. Then, on the third and the fourth days, He created the beautiful blue sky that leads up to the heavens.

Finally, on the fifth and the sixth days, Allah finished creating all the land and the mountains, hills, valleys, forests and jungles.

Allah made the Earth so that it looked beautiful from near and from far. The blue oceans sparkled and the white clouds swirled over the land and sea. Allah also created amazing sunsets, diving dolphins and lush, green rainforests. Everything on our Earth, from the great whales in the sea, to the tiny insects on the land, was created by Allah.

Then Allah made His next amazing creation – a man and a woman. He named this first man and woman Adam and Eve, and He made them from the clay of the Earth.

▲ The magnificent Grand Canyon in Arizona, USA has been shaped by the Colorado River for the past 40 million years.

Perfect Earth

Muslims believe that the Earth was specially designed for human beings to live on. They also believe that Allah created everything on Earth to work together to give all people a perfect place in which to live.

▲ Tropical rainforests are some of the most colourful and beautiful places on Earth.

Rainforests

Amongst Allah's most amazing creations on Earth is the area in South America called the Amazon. It contains more than half of all the world's rainforests. The Amazon is also the home of 75,000 types of trees, 150,000 species of plants and thousands of animals and reptiles.

At first, Allah sent Adam and Eve to live in the Garden of Eden, a very special place, full of lovely things to see and delicious food to eat. In the garden was a fruit tree full of juicy, colourful fruit.

"You must not touch the fruit that grows on this tree," Allah warned Adam and Eve. But the devil **tempted** Adam and Eve to disobey Allah and they ate some fruit from the tree. Allah knew that Adam and Eve had disobeyed Him. And because of this sin, Allah sent Adam and Eve away from the Garden of Eden to live on Earth.

Allah told Adam and Eve that on Earth they must find their own food. He also told them that the time they spent on Earth would be a test to see if they could obey Him and not do bad things.

To make the test even more difficult, Allah sent the devil to live on Earth with Adam and Eve.

Before they left the Garden of Eden, Allah warned Adam and Eve. "The devil is evil and he will tempt you to commit many more sins. You must try to resist."

The devil was very, very bad. He rubbed his hands together gleefully when Allah told him he was to stay on Earth. "I will try my best to make Adam and Eve do and say bad things and turn against you," he laughed.

With that, the devil promised to stay on Earth forever and carry on tempting all the people who lived there to do and say bad things – and this is exactly what the devil is doing every day.

✷ Allah sent Adam and Eve out of the Garden of Eden to live the rest of their lives on Earth. Here they had to learn to work the land and grow their own food.

The Angel Jibril and the Cave on Mount Hira

Muslims believe that the **Prophet** Muhammad (pbuh) was the last in a long line of prophets who were sent to the world by Allah. Prophet Muhammad (pbuh) was chosen by Allah to bring the message of Islam to the world.

When Prophet Muhammad (pbuh) was 40 years old, he was married to a woman named Khadijah. They both lived happily in the city of **Makkah** but Muhammad (pbuh) always felt that there was more to his life than what he was doing.

☪ The Prophet Muhammad (pbuh) first received the words of Allah from the Angel Jibril in the cave on Mount Hira.

Muhammad (pbuh) left the city whenever he could to climb a hill called Mount Hira. There he would sit alone at the mouth of a cave. From here he could see the whole city in the distance. The magnificent scene always made him wonder how everything had been created. What was the purpose of it all?

Muhammad (pbuh) thought about the people of Makkah, and the clay statues that they worshipped. The people believed that the statues were the gods that had created everything. But Muhammad (pbuh) could not accept that shapes made out of clay could be worshipped, and he asked for help.

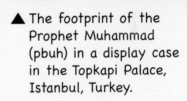

▲ The footprint of the Prophet Muhammad (pbuh) in a display case in the Topkapi Palace, Istanbul, Turkey.

Famous footprint

The Topkapi Palace in Istanbul, Turkey, has on display a number of items relating to the Prophet Muhammad (pbuh). These include a bamboo bow, a letter, some hairs from his beard and a footprint. The footprint has been set in marble.

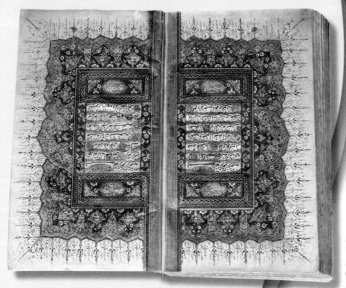

▲ The Qur'an is written in Arabic, which is read from right to left.

The Qur'an

The **Qur'an** is the book that contains the verses revealed to Prophet Muhammad (pbuh) by the Angel Jibril (Gabriel). It was revealed verse by verse over 23 years to the Prophet (pbuh). Early copies of the Qur'an are beautifully decorated using different coloured inks and even gold or silver leaf.

One night, during the month that would become the holy month of **Ramadan**, when Muhammad (pbuh) was on Mount Hira watching the sunset, he fell asleep. Suddenly, he was woken by a blinding light that surrounded him and the whole mountain. The rays of light covered the sky in different colours, and at the centre he saw the **Angel Jibril** (Gabriel). Jibril began to speak the words, "Read!"

Muhammad (pbuh) could not understand what was happening. "I cannot read," he replied, trembling with fear. Then Jibril embraced him three times, repeating the word "Read!" and Muhammad (pbuh) realised that the angel wanted him to repeat the words after him.

So Muhammad (pbuh) began to recite: "Read! In the Name of your Lord, who has created man. Read! Your Lord is the Most Generous, who has taught the skill of writing with a pen, and who has taught man that which he never knew before!"

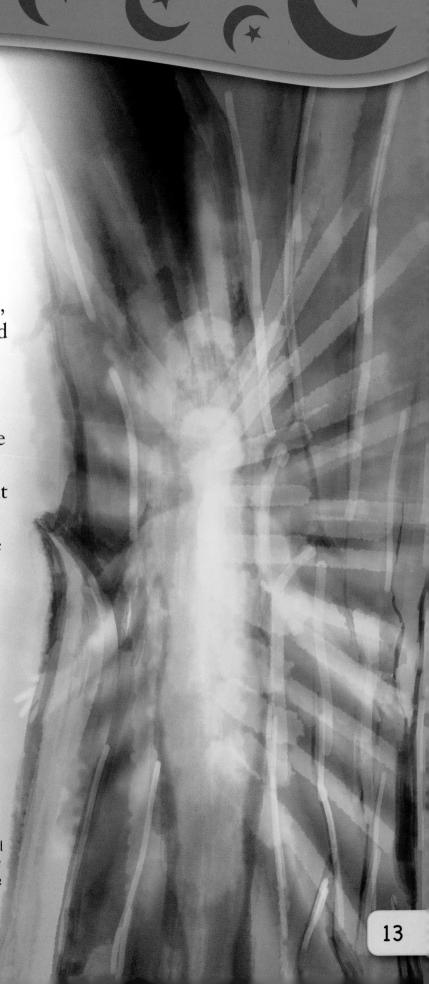

Then the angel told Muhammad (pbuh) that he had been chosen by Allah to be His final messenger.

For 23 years after first meeting the Angel Jibril, the Prophet Muhammad (pbuh) returned again and again to the mountain to hear the words of Allah that were told to him through Jibril. Each time he went back to Makkah he told his companions what he had heard and they wrote down each word.

This writing became the Qur'an, the holy book of all Muslims and of Islam.

The appearance of the Angel Jibril covered the whole sky with bright light, waking the Prophet Muhammad (pbuh) from his sleep.

An Orphan's Eid

It was the morning of **Eid ul-Fitr**. This is the day of celebration for all Muslims that comes at the end of the month of **Ramadan**, the month of fasting. The streets of the city of **Medinah** were filled with people dressed in their best clothes. They were gathering at the place that had been chosen for prayers.

The young boy Zuhair Bin Saghir was curled up alone on the side of the street when the **Prophet** Muhammad and his companions found him.

That day the Prophet Muhammad (pbuh) was to lead the special prayers. Afterwards, as the Prophet was walking home, he noticed a small, lonely person curled up by the side of the road. The Prophet went up to the figure wrapped in what looked like old rags. Coming closer, he could see that it was a small child who was crying.

The Prophet was overcome with sadness, and tears fell from his eyes at the sight of a child who had no new clothes, gifts or anything to eat on this day of happiness and celebration.

"Why are you crying?" asked the Prophet softly.

"Go away and leave me alone!" snapped the child, rudely.

The Prophet Muhammad (pbuh) sat down next to the child who still had his face hidden in his ragged cloak.

"Why are you all alone and so sad on this special day?" the Prophet asked the boy.

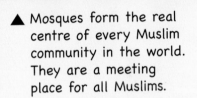

▲ Mosques form the real centre of every Muslim community in the world. They are a meeting place for all Muslims.

Special day

The main event of Eid ul-Fitr is the special Eid prayer that takes place in the mosques in the morning. All Muslims are expected to wear their best clothes on this day. Then, after the prayer, everyone meets to share the happiness of this day. Families then celebrate at home enjoying specially prepared food.

▲ The festival of Eid ul-Fitr is special for children who enjoy making Eid cards for their family and friends, exchanging gifts and wearing new clothes.

Eid ul-Fitr

Eid is an Arabic word that means "happiness", and the festival of Eid ul-Fitr is a time of great joy and celebration. Muslims thank Allah for giving them the strength to fast during Ramadan, and also ask Him to forgive them for all the bad things they have done. Many Muslims send each other special Eid cards, which are decorated with words from the **Qur'an**.

"I am an **orphan**," the boy sobbed without looking up. "My father was killed in a war and my mother married again. My new father doesn't want me, so I ran away."

"Tell me your name," said the Prophet kindly.

"My name is Zuhair Bin Saghir. Today is Eid, and everyone is happy. All the children have new clothes and nice things to eat, but I don't have any clothes except what I am wearing. I have no food and I don't have anywhere to live." The boy's skinny shoulders shook as he sobbed even harder.

The Prophet replied quietly. "I am an orphan, too. I lost my mother and father when I was a small child just like you."

Surprised at what the Prophet said, the boy slowly looked up to see who this man was. The little boy's face was covered in dirt. His chin was grazed and red from where he had fallen.

Zuhair gasped when he saw the Prophet. He recognised him immediately and sprang to his feet. The boy felt ashamed at having spoken so rudely and stood quietly with his head lowered.

The Prophet Muhammad (pbuh) smiled. "If I were to become your new father, and my wife, your new mother, and Fatimah, your new sister, would that make you feel better?" he asked the boy.

"Oh yes!" the boy cried. "That would be the best thing in the world!" And the boy looked really happy for the first time in many weeks.

The Prophet took Zuhair home and gave him new clothes and good food. The boy's new life began on this special day.

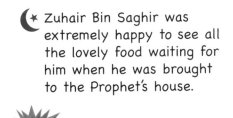
☪ Zuhair Bin Saghir was extremely happy to see all the lovely food waiting for him when he was brought to the Prophet's house.

Yusuf the Teller of Dreams

The **Prophet** Yaqub (Jacob) had 12 sons. He loved them all dearly but one son was a little different from the others. His name was Yusuf (Joseph) and he was always the best behaved, the most helpful and the best looking of the brothers. But the most interesting thing about Yusef was that he had lots of amazing dreams.

☪ Prophet Yusuf had a dream that the sun, the moon and 11 stars all bowed to him. This was a sign of how special he was going to be.

"Father, my dream last night was very strange," Yusuf said one day. "I saw 11 stars, the sun and the moon and they all bowed down to me. What do you think this means?"

On hearing this Yaqub was sure that great things were in store for his special son but told him, "Yusuf, never tell your brothers about this dream. They may become angry and **jealous**."

As time passed, this is indeed what happened. Yusuf's brothers became very jealous of Yusuf and decided to get rid of him. One day, they took Yusuf off to play near a well and then they threw him in! The brothers ran home and told their father that Yusuf had been stolen by wolves.

For days Yusuf remained trapped in the well, praying to Allah for help. A few days later, some merchants on their way to Egypt passed the well and rescued Yusuf. Amazed at his beauty, they decided to take him to Egypt to sell him as a slave.

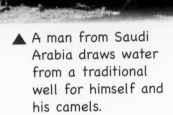

▲ A man from Saudi Arabia draws water from a traditional well for himself and his camels.

Getting water

Houses in Arabia and other parts of the Middle East used to be made of mud bricks, which kept them cool inside. There were no taps for water inside these houses. Wells were dotted around the villages and towns where the people would go to fetch water.

▲ Farmers in Saudi Arabia, in the Middle East, cut and thresh corn in the same way that it was done hundreds of years ago.

Gathering the harvest

Before machines were invented to cut and gather the harvest, the job was usually done by hand. Farmers used long curved tools called sickles to cut the corn stalks. The corn was then made into bread to feed all the families in the villages and cities.

Yusuf was sold to a man who kept him as a servant. The man's wife took a liking to Yusuf because he was so good looking, but later they quarrelled and the woman had Yusuf thrown into a dungeon. Yusuf became known by the other prisoners as the man who could explain the meaning of dreams.

At that time, the king of Egypt had a strange dream that troubled him. He saw himself on the banks of the River Nile. The water was turning into mud as he watched. Then seven fat cows came out of the river followed by seven thin cows. The seven thin cows gobbled up the seven fat ones, and the wheat that was growing on the riverbank disappeared into the mud.

☾ The merchants carried the Prophet Yusuf to Egypt, believing they would sell him as a slave for a high price.

The king asked if there was anyone who could tell him what the dream meant. They quickly brought Yusuf before the king.

"My lord," Yusuf said, "your dream means that for the next seven years Egypt will have lots of food and wealth, but for seven years after, Egypt will have **drought** and there will be very little food."

Knowing this, the king made a plan: they must store away as much food as possible to see them through the drought. "Yusef, you have helped to stop a major disaster in my kingdom," said the king. "As a reward, I am going to put you in charge of Egypt's great food stores."

When the drought came, many people, including Yusef's brothers, came to Yusuf for food, but they did not recognise him. However, Yusuf knew his brothers, and although they had tried to kill him, Yusuf missed them and longed to tell them who he was.

One day, Yusuf told them who he was. The brothers fell to the ground weeping with joy and asking for forgiveness. Yusuf was very happy to have his brothers back again and forgave them all. Later, the brothers returned to Egypt, and the family was reunited at last. They all lived together in peace and the brothers were never jealous of Yusuf again.

Prophet Sulaiman and the Queen of Saba

This is the story of another of Allah's prophets, whose name was **Prophet** Sulaiman (Solomon). Allah gave Sulaiman the amazing gift of being able to understand the language of all animals.

(The Prophet Sulaiman was very wise. He could also speak to all animals, including birds and insects.

Sulaiman had everything that any person could want, yet in spite of his wisdom and wealth, he never forgot Allah. He always told his people, "Thank Allah for everything that He has given you. Worship Allah and always do good deeds."

One day, Sulaiman was sitting on the branch of a large tree. He called all the birds to gather around him, but as he looked at the flock, he noticed that the Hoopoe bird was not there.

Suddenly, the Hoopoe bird came flying in and perched next to him. "I have come from a city far away called Saba," the Hoopoe said. "The people there are rich and they have a queen who sits on a magnificent golden throne. These people worship the sun and treat the sun as god."

Sulaiman decided to write a letter to the Queen of Saba and asked the Hoopoe to take it to her. When the Queen received the letter, she called all the wise men of the city to her.

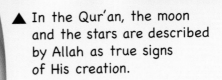

▲ In the Qur'an, the moon and the stars are described by Allah as true signs of His creation.

The moon and the stars

The moon and the stars are closely connected to Islam in a number of ways. It is said that the Prophet Muhammad (pbuh) often used to draw them with his cane on sand. The moon marks the beginning and ending of the holy month of **Ramadan**. It is also the sighting of the moon that helps Muslims to decide when the Hajj (pilgrimage to **Makkah**) should begin each year.

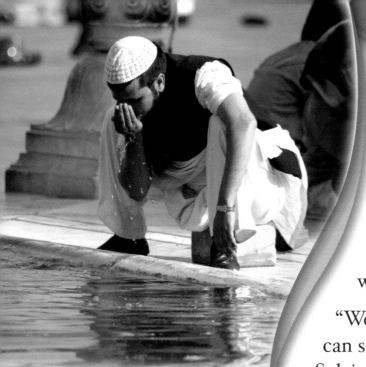

▲ Most mosques have a special place where Muslims can wash before they pray.

Preparing to pray

Before prayer, Muslims must wash in a special way called *wudu*. This is an Arabic word meaning "cleanliness". Only then can they perform Salah (the prayers that Muslims are supposed to perform five times a day). Wudu consists mainly of cleaning all the parts of the body that will come into contact with the ground while praying, such as the face, hands, arms, head and feet.

"I have received a letter from Sulaiman," said the Queen. "In it, he has written we should believe in Allah and worship only Him. What would you advise me to do?"

"We are very powerful and can send a mighty army against Sulaiman but you have to decide yourself what is to be done," the wise men answered.

"A war could destroy our city, and our best warriors will turn into cruel fighters," said the Queen. "Therefore, I would prefer not to make war. Instead, I will send Sulaiman a wonderful present."

☾★ The Queen of Saba travelled across the desert by camel to see Prophet Sulaiman.

When the Queen of Saba's messengers reached Sulaiman they gave him the Queen's present, which was a great chest full of jewels. They were very surprised when Sulaiman became angry.

"Why do you bring me these riches instead of listening to my advice?" Sulaiman said. "What Allah has given me is far better than all this. Go back to your Queen and take this chest with you!"

The Queen of Saba wondered how anyone could have refused such a valuable gift and decided to go and see Sulaiman for herself.

When the Queen arrived, Sulaiman spoke to her about Allah. He explained how everything was created by Allah and controlled by Him. The Queen slowly began to realise how wrong she had been to worship the sun.

"You are right," she told Sulaiman. "From now on, I shall worship only Allah. I will take this message back to my people so that they may also accept Allah as their Lord. He alone is our Lord and we should obey only Him."

Prophet Musa Meets a Wise Man

One day, Allah told His **prophet** Musa to go on a journey and to take a young student with him. Allah said to Musa, "On your way you will meet a wise man named Al-Khidr. You must ask Al-Khidr if you and the student can go with him on his travels, to learn from him."

So Musa and the young student set off. Not long after, they met a man who said he was Al-Khidr. The Prophet Musa asked Al-Khidr if they could travel with him and learn from his wisdom.

"Yes, you can come with me," Al-Khidr replied, "but you must not question what I do, whatever it may be, or I will go on without you." Musa agreed and the three set off on their journey.

The Prophet Musa, his student and the wise man Al-Khidr began their travels by ship.

26

As they walked along a riverbank, they saw a ship and asked the captain if they could come on board. The captain agreed.

As they set sail Al-Khidr began to pull up a plank from the bottom of the boat and water started leaking in, making it dangerous for anyone to sail in it. Prophet Musa was so surprised that he forgot his promise to remain silent and asked Al-Khidr why he had damaged the boat. But Al-Khidr reminded Musa that he must remain quiet and be **patient**. Prophet Musa apologised and, on reaching land again, they left the ship.

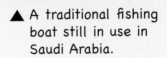

▲ A traditional fishing boat still in use in Saudi Arabia.

Fish for sale

The fish caught by fishermen in and around Saudi Arabia have always been a main source of food for Arabic people. Fishing is still a way of making a living there today. Fishermen go out in their boats in the early morning and then take the fresh fish to special markets. These are very lively places, where the fish is sold and taken to all the cities and smaller towns in the region.

▲ Gifts of food and money given by Muslims during the festival of **Eid ul-Fitr** are known as Zakat.

Giving to the needy

A very important part of every Muslim's life is giving to the poor and the needy. As part of the celebration of Eid ul-Fitr, Muslims offer food and water to the poor. Also everyone must give some of their money to charity each year.

Later the three travellers came to a city, where they asked for food. But the people told them, "If you want food, you must pay for it." The travellers had no money, so they left.

As they were walking out of the city, Al-Khidr saw a crumbling wall. He walked up to the wall and raised his hands. As soon as he did this the wall became strong again. Once more Prophet Musa questioned Al-Khidr, "Why did you repair the wall, when the people in the city refused to give us food?"

This time, Al-Khidr said, "I warned you that if you questioned what I do, I would continue on my way without you. So now I must leave, but before I go, I will explain a few things to you.

"I damaged the boat because if I had not, the king, who lives on the other side of the great river, would have taken the boat for himself.

"I know that the owners of this boat are very poor. They would not have been able to buy another boat, but they can easily repair the damage that I did.

"I repaired the wall in the city because beneath it is hidden a treasure that belongs to two orphans. The orphans are not yet old enough to have the treasure. It is better that the wall is repaired so no one will find and steal the treasure before the orphans are old enough to dig it up themselves."

The Prophet Musa and his student learned a valuable lesson from Al-Khidr, who Allah created to teach the prophets. Al-Khidr taught them that Allah sometimes makes things happen that seem to be wrong, but later we realise that it was all for the best.

Al-Khidr raised his arms to repair the crumbling city wall instantly.

Glossary

Angel Jibril (Gabriel) – the angel who first brought the message of the Qur'an to the Prophet Muhammad (pbuh)

drought – period when there has been no rain for a long time and everywhere is very, very dry

Eid ul-Fitr – the special day that comes at the end of the month of Ramadan when all Muslims fast. *Fitr* means "to break the fast" in the Arabic language.

fast – go without food or drink. Muslims fast from sunrise to sunset during the month of Ramadan

Five Pillars of Islam – the five duties that Muslims follow in their daily lives. These are: Shahadah (a declaration of faith – to say there is no God but Allah and that the Prophet Muhammad (pbuh) is his messenger), Salah (to pray), Sawm (fasting), Hajj (to go on a pilgrimage to Makkah) and Zakah (to give to charity).

jealous – feel anger because you want something that belongs to someone else

Medinah – a city in Saudi Arabia and the second holiest city in Islam. It is also the place where Prophet Muhammad (pbuh) built his mosque and where he was buried.

Makkah – the city in Saudi Arabia where Islam began, sometimes spelt Mecca

orphan – child whose parents have died

patient – able to wait for something or someone without becoming angry or upset

pilgrimage – the journey to Makkah (called Hajj) that all Muslims must make at least once in their lives if they can

Prophet – a person chosen by Allah to spread the message of Islam to people of the world

Qur'an – the holy book of Islam that contains the teachings of Allah that were given to Muhammad (pbuh)

Ramadan – the month of the year when Muslims are supposed to fast each day

tempt – try to make someone do something wrong or unwise

Find out more

Websites

www.islamicplayground.com
A website full of games, quizzes, puzzles and stories
for children.

juniors.reonline.org.uk/juniors_search.php
Lots of valuable information about Islam. The site includes
themes, topics and keywords.

atschool.eduweb.co.uk/carolrb/islam/islamintro.html
A general, colourful site for children on all aspects of Islam.

Books

Goodword Arabic Writing Book 2 by Muhammad Imran Erfani
by M. Harun Rashid
Publisher: Goodword Books, India, 2007

My Belief: I Am a Muslim by Manju Aggarwal
Publisher: Franklin Watts, 2001

Stories from Faiths: The Great Night Journey and Other Stories
by Anita Ganeri
Publisher: QED Publishing, 2007

Tell Me About the Prophet Muhammad by Saniyasnain Khan
Publisher: Goodword Books, India, 2004

Index